anythink

What are the Branches of Democracy?

Ann H. Matzke

rourkeeducationalmedia.com

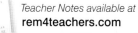

Teacher Notes available at
rem4teachers.com

www.rourkeeducationalmedia.com

PHOTO CREDITS: Cover: © t_kimura, Diana Walters, Alan Crosthwaite; Title Page, Page 11: © Lawrence Jackson; Page 3: © GYI NSEA; Page 4: © Library of Congress; Page 5: © Royce DeGrie; Page 6: © Shane Obrien, iconeer; Page 7: © iconeer; Page 8, 12, 13, 17, 18, 19: © AP Images; Page 9: © Jeremy Edwards; Page 10: © U.S. Senate, 111th Congress, Senate Photo Studio; Page 14: © Wikipedia; Page 15: © WilliamSherman; Page 16: © ihsanyildizli; Page 20, 21: © Gene Chutka;

Edited by: Precious McKenzie
Cover design by: Tara Raymo
Interior design by: Renee Brady

Library of Congress PCN Data

What are the Branches of Democracy?/Ann H. Matzke
(Little World Social Studies)
ISBN 978-1-61810-146-4(hard cover)(alk. paper)
ISBN 978-1-61810-279-9(soft cover)
Library of Congress Control Number: 2011945873

Rourke Educational Media
Printed in the United States of America,
North Mankato, Minnesota

rourkeeducationalmedia.com
customerservice@rourkeeducationalmedia.com • PO Box 643328 Vero Beach, Florida 32964

In the United States, we **elect** people to run our government and make our **laws**. This type of government is called a democracy.

The Constitution sets the rules for our government and explains **rights** and freedoms.

George Washington was a delegate to the Continental Congress.

We the People of the United States, in order to form a more perfect Union, establish Justice, insure domestic Tranquility, provide for the common defence, promote the general Welfare, and secure the Blessings of Liberty to ourselves and our Posterity, do ordain and establish this Constitution for the United States of America.

Article. I.

Section. 1. All legislative Powers herein granted shall be vested in a Congress of the United States, which shall consist of a Senate and House of Representatives.

Section. 2. The House of Representatives shall be composed of Members chosen every second Year by the People of the several States, and the Electors in each State shall have the Qualifications requisite for Electors of the most numerous Branch of the State Legislature.

No Person shall be a Representative who shall not have attained to the Age of twenty five Years, and been seven Years a Citizen of the United States, and who shall not, when elected, be an Inhabitant of that State in which he shall be chosen.

Representatives and direct Taxes shall be apportioned among the several States which may be included within this Union, according to their respective Numbers, which shall be determined by adding to the whole Number of free Persons, including those bound to Service for a Term of Years, and excluding Indians not taxed, three fifths of all other Persons. The actual Enumeration shall be made within three Years after the first Meeting of the Congress of the United States, and within every subsequent Term of ten Years, in such Manner as they shall by Law direct. The Number of Representatives shall not exceed one for every thirty Thousand, but each State shall have at Least one Representative; and until such enumeration shall be made, the State of New Hampshire shall be entitled to chuse three, Massachusetts eight, Rhode Island and Providence Plantations one, Connecticut five, New York six, New Jersey four, Pennsylvania eight, Delaware one, Maryland six, Virginia ten, North Carolina five, South Carolina five, and Georgia three.

When vacancies happen in the Representation from any State, the Executive Authority thereof shall issue Writs of Election to fill such Vacancies.

The House of Representatives shall chuse their Speaker and other Officers; and shall have the sole Power of Impeachment.

Section. 3. The Senate of the United States shall be composed of two Senators from each State, chosen by the Legislature thereof, for six Years; and each Senator shall have one Vote.

Immediately after they shall be assembled in Consequence of the first Election, they shall be divided as equally as may be into three Classes. The Seats of the Senators of the first Class shall be vacated at the Expiration of the second Year, of the second Class at the Expiration of the fourth Year, and of the third Class at the Expiration of the sixth Year, so that one third may be chosen every second Year; and if Vacancies happen by Resignation, or otherwise, during the Recess of the Legislature of any State, the Executive thereof may make temporary Appointments until the next Meeting of the Legislature, which shall then fill such Vacancies.

No Person shall be a Senator who shall not have attained to the Age of thirty Years, and been nine Years a Citizen of the United States, and who shall not, when elected, be an Inhabitant of that State for which he shall be chosen.

The Vice President of the United States shall be President of the Senate, but shall have no Vote, unless they be equally divided.

The Senate shall chuse their other Officers, and also a President pro tempore, in the Absence of the Vice President, or when he shall exercise the Office of President of the United States.

The Senate shall have the sole Power to try all Impeachments. When sitting for that Purpose, they shall be on Oath or Affirmation. When the President of the United States is tried, the Chief Justice shall preside: And no Person shall be convicted without the Concurrence of two thirds of the Members present.

Judgment in Cases of Impeachment shall not extend further than to removal from Office, and disqualification to hold and enjoy any Office of honor, Trust or Profit under the United States: but the Party convicted shall nevertheless be liable and subject to Indictment, Trial, Judgment and Punishment, according to Law.

Section. 4. The Times, Places and Manner of holding Elections for Senators and Representatives, shall be prescribed in each State by the Legislature thereof; but the Congress may at any time by Law make or alter such Regulations, except as to the Places of chusing Senators.

The Congress shall assemble at least once in every Year, and such Meeting shall be on the first Monday in December, unless they shall by Law appoint a different Day.

Section. 5. Each House shall be the Judge of the Elections, Returns and Qualifications of its own Members, and a Majority of each shall constitute a Quorum to do Business; but a smaller Number may adjourn from day to day, and may be authorized to compel the Attendance of absent Members, in such Manner, and under such Penalties as each House may provide.

Each House may determine the Rules of its Proceedings, punish its Members for disorderly Behaviour, and, with the Concurrence of two thirds, expel a Member.

Democracy Fact

In 1787, fifty-five delegates called the Continental Congress, met to write the U.S. Constitution.

5

The Constitution divides our government into three parts, or branches.

Three Branches of the Government

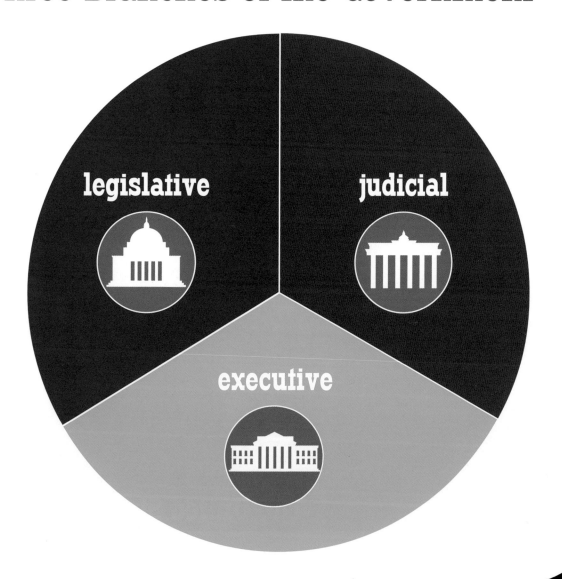

legislative

judicial

executive

Congress is the legislative branch that makes the laws.

The United States Congress

The Congress gathers in the Capitol building to make the laws for the nation.

Congress is divided into the Senate and the House of Representatives. Each group helps to write and vote on the laws.

The United States Senate

Democracy Fact

In the United States there are 435 Representatives in the House of Representatives and 100 Senators in the Senate. Representatives are determined by population. But each state has just 2 Senators.

The president is the leader of the executive branch and he approves the laws.

The president is in charge of the **armed forces**, which keep our country safe.

Army

Navy

Air Force

Marine Corps

Coast Guard

Democracy Fact
The armed forces include: the Army, Navy, Air Force, Marine Corps, and Coast Guard.

Our **court system** is part of the judicial branch which makes sure the laws are correct and used fairly.

The United States Supreme Courthouse

Democracy Fact

When Congress passes a new law the president must approve it.

Each branch is a part of a system of checks and balances so no branch has too much power.

18

Our three branches of government protect our rights as free people of the United States.

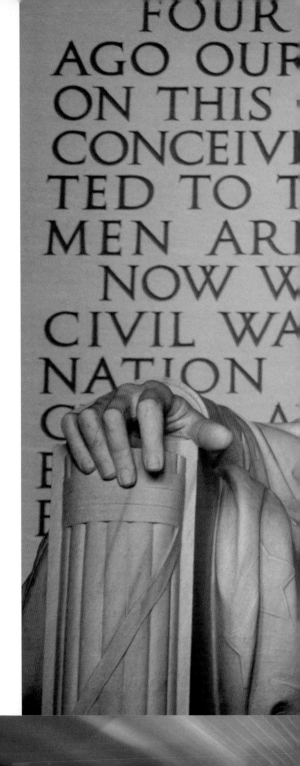

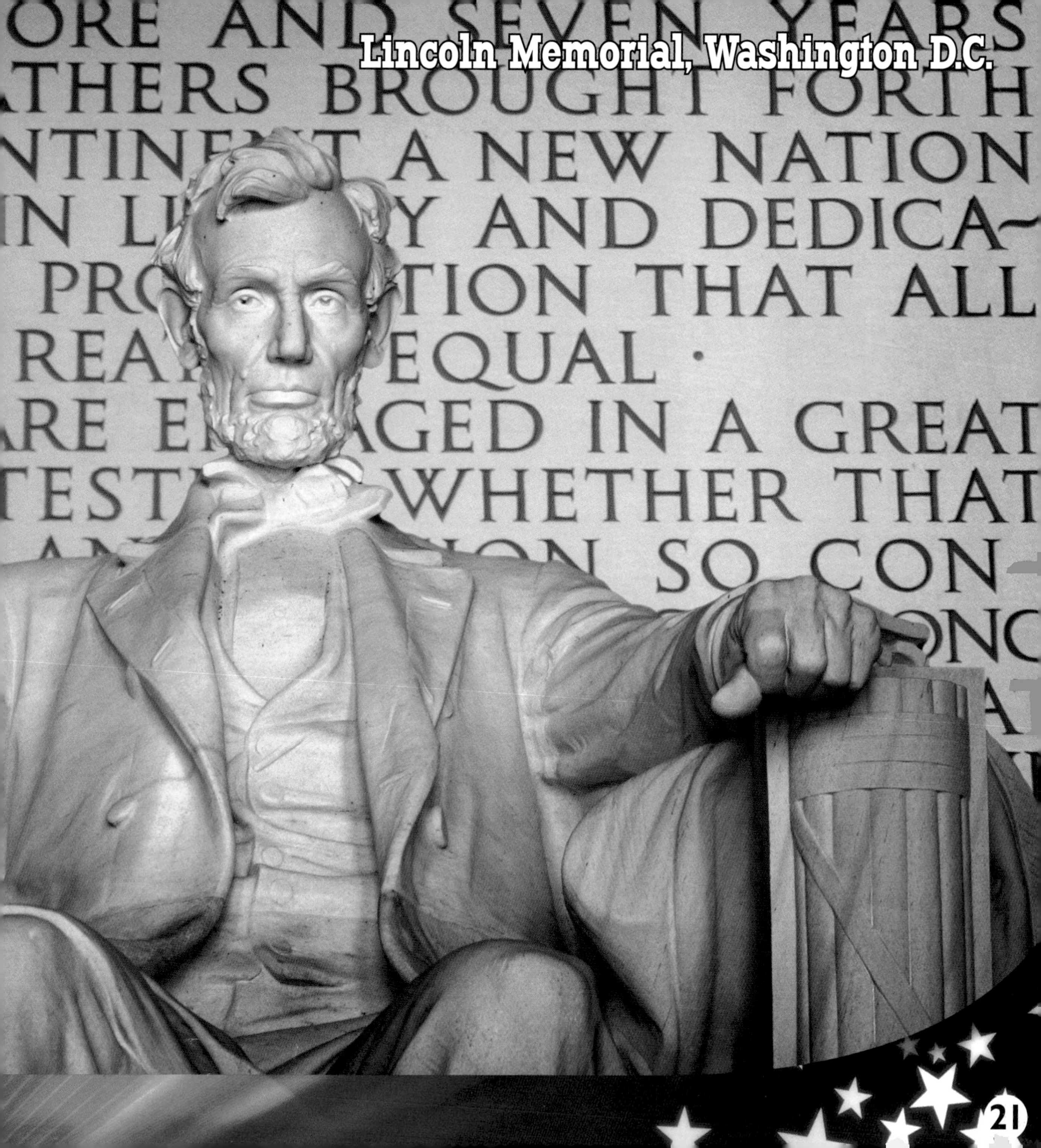

Lincoln Memorial, Washington D.C.

Picture Glossary

armed forces (armed forss-is): The different types of military that serve our country.

court (kort): Place where legal cases are heard and decided.

elect (i-LEKT): To choose someone or decide something by voting.

 **laws** (lawz): Rules made by the government that must be obeyed.

 **rights** (rites): Something the law says you can have or do.

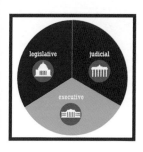 **system** (SISS-tuhm): Orderly way of doing something.

Index

Websites

pbskids.org/democracy/govandme/

kids.clerk.house.gov/

www.congressforkids.net/

About the Author

Ann H. Matzke is a children's librarian. She has an MFA in Writing for children and young adults from Hamline University. Ann lives with her family in Gothenburg, Nebraska. Nebraska is the only state to have a one-house legislature called a Unicameral. Ann enjoys traveling, reading, and writing books for children.

Ask The Author!
www.rem4students.com